Puerto Rico

Island in the Sun

A roadside fruit vendor awaits his customers along the highway to Fajardo.

Puerto Rico

Island in the Sun

Text and photographs

Roger A. LaBrucherie

Imágenes Press

*T*he twin spires of Ponce's Cathedral of Nuestra Señora de la Guadalupe glisten in the afternoon sun.

Introduction

Island in the Sun. The phrase conjures up beaches, palm trees swaying in the wind, and warm tropical waters. Puerto Rico is that, of course, but it is also much more: an island rich in history, which Columbus "discovered" and claimed for Spain on November 19, 1493, when it had already been home to indigenous peoples for some 2500 years, if the archaeologists have it right. (Columbus's visit in 1493 was, by the way, the only time and place where the Admiral of the Ocean Seas set foot on what is today American soil.)

Puerto Rico is also home to more than four million people resident on the island, as well as "home" in the sentimental sense to an equal or greater number of Puerto Ricans resident on the American mainland and elsewhere in the world. Anyone who has encountered Puerto Ricans abroad knows that they have a pride in and attachment to their homeland perhaps unequalled—and certainly unsurpassed—by any people anywhere. Spending time on the island makes it easy to see and understand why. For not only is Puerto Rico blessed with both extraordinary natural beauty and a superbly livable climate; in addition, the people of the island have a warmth, gentleness of spirit, and appreciation of family and community which can best be summed up as a zest for life. This *joie de vivre* is reflected in their love of music, the fiesta, and the island's easy informality (nowhere else in the Spanish-speaking world, I think, is the formal form of "you," *usted*, so rarely heard).

At about 100 miles long by 35 miles wide (3435 square miles), Puerto Rico is the fourth-largest of the Caribbean islands (after Cuba, neighboring Hispaniola, and Jamaica). But though located within the tropics, it would be a mistake to think of the island's climate as strictly tropical. Many of the island's towns, and much of its unspoiled beauty, are to be found in the Cordillera Central, the central "backbone" of the island, with elevations around 3000 feet (just south of Jayuya, Cerro de Punta, the highest point on the island, boasts an elevation of 4389 feet). These highlands enjoy a coolness (morning fog is common in the interior valleys) which has made them a favorite weekend and summer retreat for much of the population living on the coastal plain. And even the coastal areas, though sometimes uncomfortably warm and humid, often feel the cooling relief of the trade winds.

It is in the Cordillera Central where much of the island's history and cultural roots are to be found as well. Indeed, until well into the 20th century, when economic opportunity beckoned, the majority of the island's people lived in the mountains, working on coffee and tobacco farms, and tending their small plots of land. The mountainous interior was home to the island's people of the soil, the *jíbaro* (HEE-bar-o), respected still for their self-reliance and hard work.

Since I have now been photographing and writing about Puerto Rico for some twenty years (the present volume is my fourth about the island), it would be foolish of me to deny that I have developed a love affair with *Borinquen* (Bor-EEN-ken), to use the affectionate term derived from the Taino Indians' name for the island. Little wonder, for Puerto Rico is a remarkable island: if this book reflects a bit of the love and affection I feel for her, it will have fulfilled its purpose.

Dawn

November 19, 1493 surely dawned like any other for the Taino (Tah-EE-no) Indians who had, for some five hundred years, inhabited Puerto Rico, the island they called *Boriquén.* But within hours their world was to change forever. For on that day Christopher Columbus, in command of 17 ships and 1500 men, on his second voyage to the New World (he would eventually make a total of four voyages to the islands of the Caribbean and the Spanish Main), happened upon Puerto Rico and claimed the island for Ferdinand and Isabela. A momentous day for the Spanish, but a fateful one for the Tainos, for they could hardly have imagined that this incredible event would mark the beginning of the end of some 25 centuries of Indian civilizations on their island home.

Fifteen years later, in 1508, the Spanish sent Juan Ponce de León to establish a colony on the island. (He did not long remain as Puerto Rico's first governor, however: four years later he left Puerto Rico to seek the "fountain of youth" in Florida.) And so began nearly four centuries of Spanish rule over the island, until, in 1898, the American flag was raised over Puerto Rico when it was ceded to the United States after the Spanish-American War.

At left: Sunrise at Punta Puerto Nuevo, on the north coast near Manatí

𝓘n El Yunque (these pages), as Puerto Rico's famed rain forest is known, the island is preserved much as it was before Columbus's arrival. The calm of beautiful Juan Diego Falls (above left) awaits deep within the forest. Here, too, the rare and endangered Puerto Rican parrot (above right), with the aid of the U. S. Fish and Wildlife Service, is making a comeback from the edge of extinction.

$\mathcal{A}$ series of indigenous peoples, culminating with the Tainos, occupied Puerto Rico for some 25 centuries before Columbus discovered the island in 1493. Relic of the 15th century, the fragment of a pot (above left) testifies to the Tainos' pottery-making skills. The restored ceremonial ball courts in the mountains near Utuado (above right) are part of the largest such complex in the Caribbean.

Sentimental symbol of the island, the tiny tree frog known as the *coquí* (ko-KEE), produces a nighttime chorus heard in almost all parts of the island. (Actual size of the *coquí* pictured on the facing page: about 3/4" in length.)

In 1539 the Spanish began building San Felipe del Morro (or as it is more simply known, "El Morro," these pages), to guard the entrance to San Juan Harbor. Part of a complex of defensive works which would eventually ring Old San Juan, the massive fortress rises some 150 feet above the sea.

*C*ompanion-piece to El Morro, 17th-century Fort San Cristóbal (facing page), the largest of all Spanish forts in the New World, provided San Juan's landward defense. Ponce de León, honored with a statue in the city's Plaza de San José (above left), was the colony's first governor before departing in search of the "fountain of youth" in Florida. Today a history museum, the Ballajá Barracks (above right) housed soldiers during the Spanish colonial era.

$\mathcal{T}$he early decades of the 20th century saw sugar cane (above) dominating the island's coastal plains, and the sugar industry dominating the island's economy. While King Sugar's fortunes declined after the Second World War, tourism began to play a major economic role. Today luxury hotels, such as the Gran Meliá on the north shore (facing page), are the stars of the island's coastline.

La Isla del Encanto

Four centuries of Spain's rule placed an indelible stamp on the island, and despite over a century as an American territory, Puerto Rico remains a profoundly Latin culture. Not that the Washington-appointed governors did not attempt to Americanize the Puerto Rican people in the early decades of the twentieth century. Indeed, part of the motivation for the Spanish-American War and the annexation of Puerto Rico in its aftermath was the firmly held notion that the United States had a manifest duty to impart the benefits of American culture to the people of the island.

It goes without saying that many tourists come to the island primarily for its sun, sea, and casinos, and that many of them never experience much of the island beyond the confines of their hotels. That is a shame; for, its scenic beauty aside, Puerto Rico offers a unique opportunity to experience a Latin American culture without ever having to leave America. There are those who belittle the island's culture, with the observation that it is just a blend of American and Latin American cultures. That is no doubt true; but the fact is that in today's world nearly *every* culture is a blend, and that blend is part of the island's charm, part of what makes Puerto Rico *la Isla del Encanto*—the Island of Enchantment.

At left: A stunning section of the north coast, with famed El Yunque Peak in the background.

*T*he Punta Tuna Light sits atop a dramatic peninsula at the southeastern corner of the island (facing page). One hundred miles to the west, the Cabo Rojo Light House overlooks the Caribbean at Puerto Rico's southwestern corner (above).

The centerpiece of each of the island's towns is its central plaza, invariably dominated by a Catholic church, a legacy of the Spanish colonial era. Porta Coeli, in San Germán (above) is the second-oldest church on the island; other striking examples are to be found at (facing page, clockwise from the top left): Moca, Vega Baja, Utuado, Hatillo, and Guayama.

On the south coast, Ponce jealously guards its architectural heritage, and the city's Plaza de las Delicias holds two gems: the Cathedral of Nuestra Señora de la Guadalupe (facing page), and, just behind the cathedral, the historic red-and-black firehouse (above).

$\int$ ome the island's most beautiful beaches line the north coast: this isolated point (above) lies just west of Fajardo. During the week, beach-goers at Playa Piñones (facing page), just east of San Juan, also find splendid isolation.

$\mathcal{M}$angrove "atolls" decorate the Caribbean near La Parguera (above). Across the island, the Mameyes River empties into the Atlantic near Luquillo (facing page).

*T*he Wyndham Río Mar Resort (facing page) at Río Grande on the
Atlantic shore between San Juan and Fajardo. Above, the marina at the
Palmas del Mar resort on the east coast near Humacao.

San Juan

My love affair with Viejo San Juan, the oldest city under the American flag, began on my very first journey to Puerto Rico. On that balmy summer evening more than thirty years ago, I walked her narrow, cobble-stoned streets with a group of my Peace Corps friends, marveling at her colorful, stuccoed facades. As the street lamps came flickering on, we found an inviting restaurant on the Plaza de San José and talked long into the night.

Only years later would I learn more about Old San Juan: although founded in 1521, most of the city's buildings date from the 18th and 19th centuries; the blue cobblestones, called *adoquines,* are actually bricks which served as ballast in the holds of ships arriving from Spain during the age of sail; the city's massive stone wall was begun in the 1600s and completely surrounded Old San Juan until the 1890s, when portions of the wall were torn down to facilitate the city's expansion. (Historic Forts San Cristóbal and El Morro and the city wall are now property protected and administered by the U.S. National Park Service.)

Today the capital is a modern, bustling city, complete with freeways, high-rise office buildings, and shopping centers, her million-plus inhabitants spread over an area many times the few hundred acres of Old San Juan. But every time I return to Puerto Rico, it is to those narrow, historic streets where I am always first drawn.

At left: A pair of cruise ships grace San Juan Harbor as evening descends over the city.

San Juan, old and new: the aerial view above takes in Viejo San Juan, as the "old city" founded by Ponce de León in 1521 is known. (The executive mansion known as "La Fortaleza" is in the foreground.) But "new" San Juan, with its "Golden Mile" including Isla Verde and Ocean Park (facing page) is as modern as any city in America.

The Alcaldía (City Hall) faces the Plaza de Armas, crossroads of Old San Juan (facing page). The daily domino game (above) has been a fixture of Old San Juan's plazas for decades.

The statue of Christopher Columbus in the Plaza de Colón (above) was erected in 1893 to commemorate the 400th anniversary of his discovery of Puerto Rico. A study in contrasts, the Fifth Centenary Plaza (facing page), was built one hundred years later, to mark the 500th anniversary of that historic event. The column is studded with terracotta artifacts uncovered during the excavation of the plaza's foundations.

These pages: Glimpses of Old San Juan's enchanting architectural heritage. The charming building shown above, at the edge of San Juan Harbor, houses a tourist information office.

Old San Juan's Cathedral of San Juan Bautista (facing page) dates from 1809. The first church on the site was erected in 1521, the year the city was founded. Modeled after the U.S. Capitol in Washington, D.C., the *capitolio* (above) houses the island's bicameral legislature.

$\mathcal{W}$hile Puerto Ricans justly celebrate their rich history, the stunning Puerto Rico Convention Center (above), the largest such facility in the Caribbean, reflects the island's intent to focus on its future as well. The Condado (facing page), together with adjacent Ocean Park and Isla Verde, collectively comprise San Juan's "Gold Coast," home to upscale condos and most of the city's first class hotels.

Island in the Sun

Among the rewards of being a photojournalist are the opportunities to travel, to meet and get to know people far removed from one's own way of life, and to see, and record for others, the extraordinary beauty of distant places.

In recent years I have begun to realize how lucky I have been, and how much I have taken for granted. Perhaps because of this, and because they are especially gorgeous to me, whenever I finish photographing a sunrise or a sunset, my last step in the process, before packing up my equipment, is to say: "Thank you, God, for giving me another beautiful day."

Puerto Ricans have been extraordinarily blessed with a gorgeous island, and I am sometimes privileged, when making aerial photographs, to see it from a low-flying airplane or helicopter. That vantage point provides another perspective as well: of the rampant, unplanned development which threatens to overwhelm what little remains of the island's unspoiled natural beauty. I fervently hope that the people of Puerto Rico will awake to the tragedy of unchecked "growth" before their island is so covered over with highways and buildings that it becomes impossible to make a photograph of a sunrise or sunset unblemished by man's hand.

At left: Playa Buyé, near the southwestern corner of the island

To the east of San Juan lies spectacular Piñones Beach (facing page). Bay grapes and coconut palms line the beach west of Cape San Juan, near Fajardo (above).

$\mathcal{C}$overing some 30,000 acres, the El Yunque Rain Forest (these pages) is a sea of green, the finest preserve of native habitat on the island. Giant tree ferns (facing page) cascade toward the Atlantic. La Coca (above left) is the most spectacular of the forest's waterfalls.

*I*n Puerto Rico's modern economy, tourism has come to play an increasingly dominant role: the spectacular El Conquistador Resort (above), perched high on a cliff near Fajardo, overlooks Palominitos and Palomino Islands (in the foreground and background, respectively, on the facing page).

*D*awn silhouettes the Cordillera Central. This mountainous backbone of the island has been home to cattle ranches, tobacco farms, and coffee plantations since the 16th century.

*S*ymbol of modern travel, a cruise ship slips past historic El Morro on its way to its berth in San Juan Harbor (above). Luquillo Beach, on the north coast, is the most famous of the island's *balnearios* (facing page).

Some twenty miles to the east of the main island lies Culebra Island, and just east of Culebra, tiny Culebrita (above), Puerto Rico's easternmost point. Some ten miles to the southwest of Culebra is Vieques (facing page), whose scalloped southern shore holds some of the most exquisite beaches in all Puerto Rico.

Sunsets on Puerto Rico's south and west coasts

Puerto Rico

Location and geography: Smallest and easternmost of the Greater Antilles, Puerto Rico lies between Hispaniola, 75 miles to the west across the Mona Passage, and the Virgin Islands, some 40 miles to the east. The island measures approximately 110 miles east to west, and 35 miles north to south. Total land area: 3435 square miles (8897 square kilometers), including its adjacent islands, of which Vieques, Culebra and Mona are the largest. The Cordillera Central, with elevations above 3,000 feet, runs east to west somewhat south of the center of the island. Highest elevation: 4389 feet (1338 meters) at Cerro de Punta.

Population: 3,944,259 (about 1148 people per square mile). Major municipalities and populations: San Juan (capital): 427,000; Bayamón: 222,000; Ponce: 181,000; Carolina: 188,000; Mayagüez: 94,000; Caguas: 143,000.

Government: Since 1952, a commonwealth in voluntary association with the United States; officially, the Commonwealth of Puerto Rico, or *Estado Libre Asociado de Puerto Rico* ("Free Associated State of Puerto Rico"), in Spanish. Essentially self-governing under the Constitution of Puerto Rico in all internal matters, although federal law governs in many areas (including the currency, post office, customs, and immigration). Universal adult suffrage elects a governor and a bicameral legislature; the judiciary completes the tripartite governmental structure. Puerto Ricans are U.S. citizens; U.S. citizens resident in Puerto Rico have no vote in federal elections and pay no federal tax on island-generated income.

Economy: Based principally on manufacturing (pharmaceuticals, electronics, clothing, textiles, etc.); the trade, finance, insurance, real estate, tourism, and agriculture sectors follow in importance. Gross domestic product per capita: $19,300.

Climate: Tropical; along the north coast the mean temperature varies from 80°F. (27°C.) in summer to 75°F. (24°C.) in winter, with about 60" (1500 mm) of rainfall distributed fairly evenly throughout the year, heaviest from May to December. The south coast is drier and somewhat warmer; the interior mountains, considerably cooler. Temperatures are moderated by the nearly constant northeasterly trade winds.

Miscellaneous: Language: Spanish; English is widely spoken. Religion: predominantly Roman Catholic, significant minority of Protestant adherents.

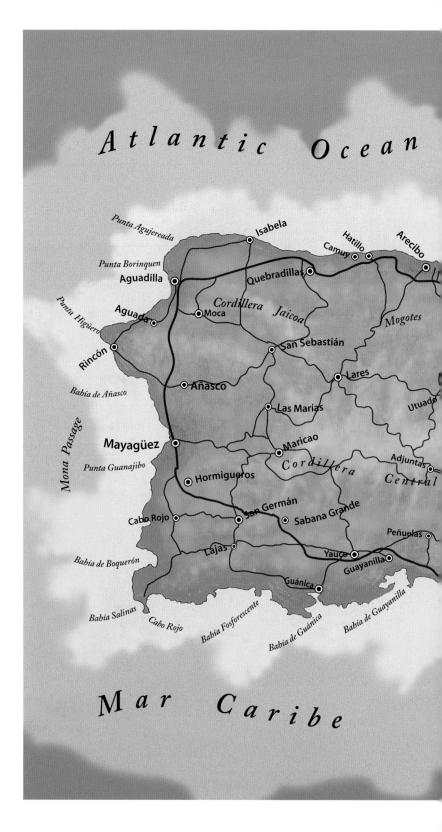

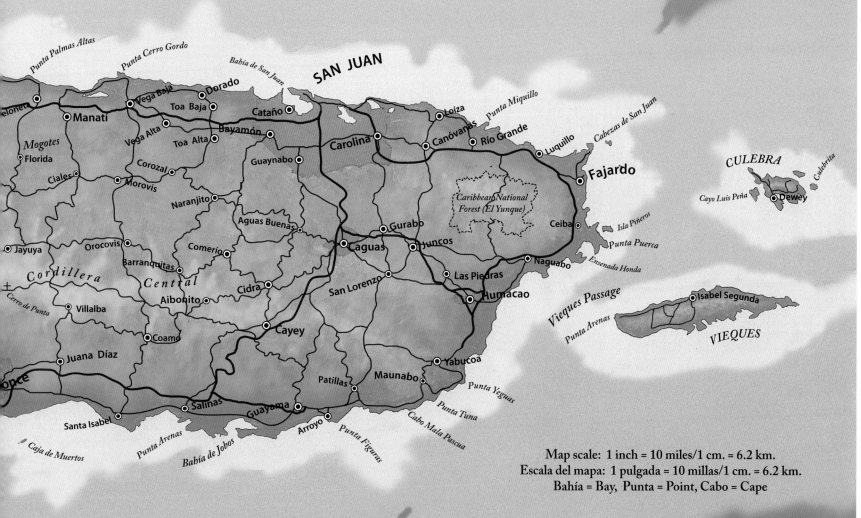

Océano Atlántico

Punta Palmas Altas
Punta Cerro Gordo
Bahía de San Juan
SAN JUAN

...elonet
Manatí
Mogotes
Florida
Ciales
Morovis
Vega Baja
Dorado
Toa Baja
Cataño
Bayamón
Vega Alta
Toa Alta
Corozal
Naranjito
Guaynabo
Carolina
Loíza
Canóvanas
Río Grande
Punta Miquillo
Luquillo
Cabezas de San Juan
Fajardo

CULEBRA
Culebrita
Cayo Luis Peña
Dewey

Jayuya
Orocovis
Barranquitas
Aguas Buenas
Comerío
Gurabo
Juncos
Caguas
Ceiba
Isla Piñeros
Punta Puerca
Ensenada Honda
Caribbean National
Forest (El Yunque)

Cordillera
Central
Cidra
San Lorenzo
Las Piedras
Naguabo

Villalba
Aibonito
Cayey
Humacao
Vieques Passage
Isabel Segunda

Cerro de Punta
Coamo
Juana Díaz
...nce
Santa Isabel
Punta Arenas
Caja de Muertos
Bahía de Jobos
Salinas
Guayama
Arroyo
Punta Figuras
Patillas
Maunabo
Yabucoa
Punta Yeguas
Punta Tuna
Cabo Mala Pascua
Punta Arenas
VIEQUES

Caribbean Sea

Map scale: 1 inch = 10 miles/1 cm. = 6.2 km.
Escala del mapa: 1 pulgada = 10 millas/1 cm. = 6.2 km.
Bahía = Bay, Punta = Point, Cabo = Cape

*T*he setting sun silhouettes a row of coconut palms near Rincón on the west coast.

Imágenes Press
Post Office Box 1150
Pine Valley, California 91962 USA
Tel: (619) 473-8676 or (619) 997-8676
Email: ImagenesPress@aol.com
or: ImagenesPress@hotmail.com
Printed in China

Puerto Rico, Island in the Sun
(Revised Edition)

ISBN13   978-0-939302-42-0
ISBN   0-939302-42-X

S. Bartholome
R. Eremoso
Salinas
Havana

Nueses I.
Matances
Pta Chrichen Xaua
Pta de Ytcos
Caio de
Sal

Panuco
R. Panuco
Colompra
Salina
I. de Lobos
La Bermeja
Negrillos
Los Alcaranes
Pta d. Ibalus
Pta Colorada
C. S. Antonio

S. An.
zines
S'ta Cruz
Havana
S. Christophore
Caio blanco

Baixos de Tuspa
R. de Casones
Medos d'Area
I. das Areas
Baixo de Sisal
P. de
Lagartos
Zuyo o
Conil
B. de Conil
C. de Cotoche
I. de Pinos
Caio blanco
Winthonts
Eylanden

U
Tameco
CO

Triangulo
La Desco
nescida
Chuaca
V. de
Mucheres
CUBA
Spaens de

ATLAS
DI
R. de S. Pedro
S. Pablo
de Almeria
Tobia
Torre branco
Merina
Caiman Grande

CALA
h Tlascala
Villa
Vic
Los Angeles
EN
R. de Santoyal
La Carca
o As Arcas
Sisal
Punta
Delgada
Yzucs
Vallanolin
IUCA.
Cozumel
Cocomes

R. de Vera Crus
Branci
Vo de Sacrificios
GOLFO DE CAMPECHE
Catqui
Coal
Telchaque
Cisle
S. Francisco
de Campeche
Lago de
Bacalal
GOLFO

Kalapa
Veracrus
Capotitlan
C. de la Vera Crus
S. Iuan De
Ulua
Sardo
R. Alvarado
Boca Partida
Sierras de S. Marin
R. de Guazacoalco
Medos d'Area
R. Real
I. Triste
R. S. Paulo
Morro dos
Diabolos
Champoton
TAN.
DE

NGEL
R. de
Zaputecas
Spiri tu Santo
HONDURAS.

Antequera
Nixapa
TABASCO
V. S. de la
Victoria
Lago de
Xicalingo
I. de
Chetumal
Zaratan
Chetumal
Quitasuenon
Santamilla o
S. Millan

GUAXACA
Tutepeque
Ciudad Real
R. de Grioba
Tibob
S. Alamana
Tamanay
Pantoja
Guanaja
I. de Leyn

DE MEXICO
Chiapa
Golfo de Guanajos
pto de Yiguens
C. de tres Puntas
Vila
Guajan
C. de Honduras
R. Grande
Guayana
Mewen Eylanden

Aquatu ico
Tocoantepec
Quizalan
SOCONUSCO
Gueyuetlan
VERA PAX.
Vera Pax
pto S. Bara
Dolura
Salmedina
Truxillo
R. Guzamen
C. de Camaron
Maven Eylanden

R. Amatlan
R. Mastatlan
AUDIENCA
DE
B. de
Cartago
o Catuski
Vitiosas

MAR
R. Colalte
R. Capanaraxte
R. Coatlan
Vulcan
S. Pedro
S. Iago De
Guatimala
Gratias
o Dios
HONDURAS.
G. de Nicuese

R. Ayula
R. Xicalapa
R. de Guatimala
La Trinidad
S. Sal
Vador
Vo de Nico
Comayagua
V. de Valid
S. Iago de Olanch
C. de gratias a Dios
R. de Vare
Bibori
Indisch
Dorpjen

GUATIMALA
S. Miguel
Segovia
Taguzcalpa
o Taguzigalpa
R. Yarepo
Yas de
Perlas

DEL ZUR
R. Lempa
B. de Fonseca
La Possession
Nequecen
Realejos
Granada
Leon
Iaen
Vulcan
NICARAGUA.
Lago de
Nicaragua
Dejuguilor
Pto de S. Iuan
R. de los Anzuelos
I. de
Manglares
S. Anden
Sta Catel

MAR